The Age of Castles

CASTLE UNDER SIEGE

Richard Dargie

WAYLAND

The Age of Castles

Titles in this series

CASTLE LIFE
CASTLE UNDER SIEGE
HOW CASTLES WERE BUILT
KNIGHTS AND CASTLES

Series editor: Alex Woolf
Editor: Jason Hook
Designer: Peter Laws
Cover Designers: Rachel Hamdi and Holly Fulbrook
Illustrator: Peter Dennis
Project artwork: John Yates
Picture research: Carron Brown
Consultant: Richard Eales, Senior Lecturer in History, University of Kent.

First published in 1998 by Wayland Publisher Ltd
This edition revised in 2007 by Wayland,
an imprint by Hachette Children's Books.

British Library Cataloguing in Publication Data
Dargie, Richard
Castle under siege. - (The age of castles)
1. Sieges- History - Juvenile literature
2. Castles - History - Juvenile literature
3. Middle Ages - Juvenile literature
I. Title II Dennis, Peter
725.1'8'0902

ISBN 978 0 7502 5201 0
Printed and bound in China
Hachette Children's Books 338 Euston Road, London NW1 3BH

PICTURE ACKNOWLEDGEMENTS
The publishers would like to thank the following for permission to publish their pictures:
(t=top; c=centre; b=bottom; l=left; r=right) AKG London *cover*, 25, 33b; Ancient Art and
Architecture 12, 14, 31, 34, 41t; Angelo Hornak 16; Copyright Richard Davis – reproduced
courtesy of The Board and Trustees of the Armouries, *Tr.2227* 19t, *Tr 2752* 21; The Board
and Trustees of the Armouries *Tr 217*, 37t, *Tr 200* 37b; © Bodleian Library, University of
Oxford, 1998, *MS.Bodley 264, part 1, 14, 113v* 15b, *MS.Bodley 264, part 1, 31, 201* 18bl,
19br; Bridgeman Art Library, London/New York, /Fitzwilliam Museum, University of
Cambridge 5, /Musée Condé, Chantilly, France, Giraudon 9, /British Library, London 11,
17tl, 36, /Castello del Buonconsiglio, Trent 13l, /Bibliotèque Nationale, Paris 18t, 19cl, 27,
32, 35t, /Palazzo Communale, Siena 22, /Lambeth Palace Library, London 30, /Musée des
Beaux-Arts, Chartres, Lauros-Giraudon 42; British Library 13tr, 15t, 35b; British Museum
13br, 29, 40, 41br; E T Archive 20, 33t; Getty Images Limited 26, 43; Michael Holford 6;
Robert Harding 7, 8, 41bl; Stock Market 23; Topham Picturepoint 39.

CONTENTS

⬚⬚⬚⬚⬚

CASTLES AND SIEGES

THE FIRST SIEGES

THE HISSING OF EXCITED GEESE wakes the slumbering Roman sentry. 'The Gauls are attacking!' he shouts to his sleeping comrades. The Romans pick up their swords and push the enemy ladders from the ramparts. The Gaulish commander curses the sacred geese. The siege of Rome has lasted seven months, and still he cannot gain victory.

Sieges were common in ancient times. In 390 BC, the city of Rome was besieged by the vast army of a Celtic people called Gauls. The Gauls burnt most of the city, but the Romans held out in their hilltop fortress called the Capitol. A legend tells how the Romans were alerted to the Gauls' night raid by the sacred geese that lived there.

△ The sacred geese save the Capitol from surprise attack.

THE TROJAN HORSE

The poet Homer tells how the ancient Greeks besieged the city of Troy for ten years. Finally, the Greek soldiers appeared to sail away, leaving behind a great wooden horse. The Trojans thought this was a gift to the gods and dragged it through their gates. At night, the Greek soldiers crept out from their hiding place inside the hollow horse and captured Troy.

In 212 BC, Roman soldiers besieged the Greeks at Syracuse in Sicily. The city's defence was masterminded by the famous scientist Archimedes. He invented new weapons of war during the siege. He is said to have used large mirrors to direct the sun's rays at Roman ships, setting them alight. Archimedes also built catapults which fired burning balls of tar.

WHAT IS A SIEGE?

The defenders feel safe in their motte and bailey castle. The Norman knights cannot spur their horses up the steep motte. They try to set fire to the wooden castle, but its walls have been soaked with water. If the defenders have enough food and water they may survive until their allies arrive. If not, they may have to surrender the keys to the castle gates.

△ Norman troops besiege the castle of Dinant, in Brittany. The defender on the right surrenders the keys to the castle gates.

Medieval leaders were sometimes afraid of meeting their enemies in open battle. Instead, they would stay in their castles and wait for the enemy to lay siege. If the castle had enough supplies, and the attackers failed to breach its walls, the siege could last for months. Eventually, the enemy might get bored and go away.

SIEGE ENGINES

By AD 1100, kings and lords had built hundreds of strong, stone castles across Europe. To try to break through their walls, attackers wheeled up enormous machines called siege engines, like this catapult or 'mangonel'. Such machines had been used in ancient times to launch all sorts of missiles, including a mysterious ball of burning flames called 'Greek fire'.

Castle defenders fought back in many different ways. In 1139, Ludlow Castle in England was besieged by King Stephen and the Scottish Prince Henry. As they walked around its walls, the defenders lowered down a grappling hook, caught hold of the prince's cloak and lifted him into the air. King Stephen managed to cut the prince free, but their siege of Ludlow Castle ended in failure.

◁ Ludlow Castle was built to defend the English border against Welsh raids.

PREPARING FOR A SIEGE

THE CASTLE

RICHARD THE LIONHEART stares proudly across the valley. On a hill, high above the River Seine, stands his new castle. The mighty Chateau Gaillard guards the roads into Richard's lands in Normandy. Now they will be safe from French attack.

King Richard I of England built Castle Gaillard to protect his lands in Normandy. Its towers had rounded edges to deflect stones from siege catapults. When Richard died, however, his brother John would not spend enough money on completing the castle. In 1204, five French knights climbed through a window and captured part of the castle.

△ Although it is in ruins today, Chateau Gaillard is still an impressive sight.

▷ A medieval king discusses the building of a castle tower with his mason.

Kings and lords hired skilled masons to build castles which could stand up to weeks of battering and bombardment. One German engineer was imprisoned after building a castle for a French duke. This was done so he could not point out the castle's weak points to the duke's enemies.

MAKE A MANGONEL

You need a hammer, thick wood (15cm x 15cm), 2 long nails, elastic band, plastic spoon.

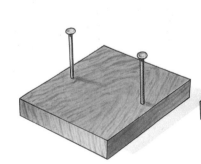

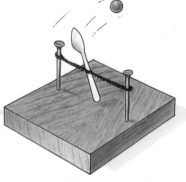

1. First hammer the nails into the wood.

2. Stretch the elastic band between the nails. Push the spoon through the band, and turn it over and over until the band is tight.

3. Place a Plasticine cannon ball on the spoon. Pull the spoon back and fire at your model castle.

A SOLDIER'S LIFE

A sergeant from the castle garrison watches a merchant using his scales. Short measures are a common cause of argument on market days. The sergeant has been ordered to keep the peace at the fair. Some of his men-at-arms check that a brewer's beer has not been watered down. Others have caught a poacher selling rabbits, and the soldiers place him in the stocks.

The castle garrison acted as the police on their lord's estate. They kept order on market days and tried to stop the village peasants from poaching the lord's game. The soldiers slept in the guardroom above the castle gates, and most of them spent their free time gambling and drinking.

△ Soldiers keep the peace at a market in the castle courtyard.

Each dawn, the castle sergeant inspected the garrison and gave the soldiers their duties for the day. The castle armoury and the stables were checked to see that everything was in order. If a siege was expected, the sergeant made sure that piles of rocks were ready as missiles.

TOLL GATES

Some castles guarded the road into a rich market town. It was the garrison's duty to collect a toll from travellers, pilgrims and merchants at the city gates. Traders had to pay this fee before they could sell their wares in the town.

THE DEFENCES

As attackers approach the castle, its gatehouse looks unprepared. The portcullis is up. The drawbridge is still down. The wooden bridge has not been set alight. But the defenders lie hidden on high wooden galleries. If the enemy soldiers enter the castle, the portcullis will fall shut behind them. They will be trapped in this 'murder hole', and will be an easy target for the castle's crossbowmen.

To prepare their castle for a siege, the defenders built wooden galleries which jutted out from the castle walls. They could drop rocks and boiling oil from these platforms on to the besiegers below. Wet leather hides were draped over these wooden fortifications so that the enemy could not set them alight.

△ This castle gate was protected by a drawbridge, a moat and a portcullis.

A QUICK HARVEST

'The French King ordered his serfs to cut down all the crops and take them into the castles. Not one single ear of grain would be left standing by the time the English army arrived.'

Everyone in the castle had to help in the preparations if a siege was expected. Trees and houses near the castle were cut down so that the enemy would find no cover or shelter. Ponds and wells were poisoned. Farmland was scorched so that nothing which the besiegers could eat would grow there.

△ Supplies of timber are carried into the castle to strengthen its fortifications.

△ Craftsmen in the castle.

Craftsmen were important during a siege. Blacksmiths made weapons while masons helped to strengthen fortifications. Before a siege started, local craftsmen were ordered to gather in the castle, so that they could not be forced to work for the besieging army.

STORES

Guarded by an enormous moat, the castle remains undefeated for weeks. While the attackers grow hungry, the occupants of the castle live off the stores in the keep. Every morning, the quartermaster gives each man his ration for the day. Three soldiers guard the cellars where the stores are kept.

△ Fougères Castle in France was protected by its moats.

Hunger and thirst were the most dangerous enemies of a besieged castle. Before a siege, the quartermaster made sure there were enough stores in the cellars. His men herded cattle into the castle for slaughter, and pickled their meat in barrels of brine. Grain was cooked into biscuit, and milk was made into cheese to make it last.

▷ The quartermaster orders local peasants to take their cattle to the castle.

A medieval book for knights said: 'If a castle is not to be forced into surrender, there must be stores of wheat, haunches of bacon, sausages, entrails and meat puddings. One needs a spring that flows continuously and underground passages for bringing in food secretly.'

SWORDS AND ARROWS

Before a siege, the castellan stocked up the castle armoury. He bought extra supplies of arrows and spears, and the blacksmiths made armour and sharpened swords on a grindstone (left). In 1204, Chateau Gaillard ran out of arrows during a siege. The castellan ordered his men to put straw dummies on the battlements, so that he could collect up the arrows fired at them by the besiegers.

THE ATTACK

TUNNELLING

BENEATH THE CASTLE, a secret enemy is at work. Miners are silently digging an underground tunnel. They burrow beneath the stone walls, where they build a great pile of logs. When these are set alight, the heat will splinter the stones above. The wall will collapse, and the castle will be captured.

rebuilt tower

When King John besieged Rochester Castle in 1215, his miners tunnelled under the south-east corner of the keep. They smeared the wooden props holding up the tunnel with the fat of forty pigs. When this was set alight, the whole tower collapsed. The tower was later rebuilt, and you can see it on the picture above. It is more rounded than the other towers.

△ The great stone keep of Rochester Castle in Kent, England.

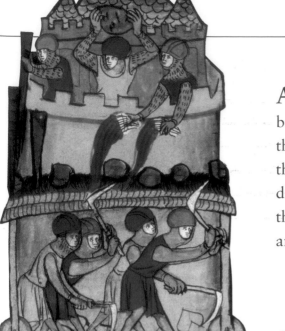

At Carcassonne Castle in France, the defenders placed bowls of water on the ground. When they saw ripples, they knew that miners were making vibrations beneath them. They drilled holes down to the enemy tunnel and dropped in oil and torches. Then, the defenders dug their own 'counter-mine', broke into the enemy tunnel and attacked the miners.

△ Miners dig out a tower's foundations, protected by a canopy from missiles dropped by the defenders.

▷ A siege engineer levers out stones from a castle's foundations. He works quietly to avoid detection.

Most miners learnt their craft in the deep iron and silver mines of Germany and Bohemia. They travelled across Europe selling their skills as siege engineers. A medieval book on building castles warned: 'Choose a site on very hard rock.'

BOMBARDING

The rope of the winch groans, as the soldiers pull down the long arm of the 'trebuchet'. A huge stone is rolled into its leather sling. They release the rope, a counterweight swings the arm upwards, and the missile flies towards the castle.

▽ Crusaders fire a trebuchet at a Muslim castle.

The trebuchet launched stone or metal balls up to two hundred metres. It could be fired with great accuracy to hit the same point in a castle wall. Battered defenders would often ride out and try to set the trebuchet alight. Besiegers also used giant crossbows called ballistas, like the one on the left, to spear men with giant arrows.

GREEK FIRE

'The Turks brought up a terrible engine of war which threw Greek Fire at us ... As it flew at us, it made such a noise as if it were a thunderbolt falling from heaven, and it seemed to me like a great dragon flying in the air.'

Jean Joinville, Sixth Crusade
1248-54.

◁ Crusaders fire the heads of prisoners during the siege of Nicaea.

△ The trebuchet was worked by the tension of the rope created by heavy weights.

In 1098, soldiers of the First Crusade besieged the castle of Nicaea in Turkey. They used trebuchets to bombard its walls with the heads of Turkish prisoners of war, in order to terrify the defenders. The Turks, not surprisingly, surrendered the next day.

In 1346, an army besieged Tana in southern Russia. Some of these besiegers died of a plague called the Black Death. Their rotting corpses were lobbed over the walls of Tana in the hope that the disease would spread to the defenders.

▷ Soldiers using a trebuchet.

SCALING AND BATTERING

The wooden siege tower rumbles along the ramp of earth that the attackers have built across the moat. Archers on the tower let fly a hail of arrows to clear the castle battlements. The tower's drawbridge crashes down on to the walls, and fifty knights rush into combat.

Attackers used siege towers to raise themselves to the height of the castle walls. The men inside operated rollers and levers to move the towers forward. Siege towers were covered in wet hides which could not be set alight. Instead, defenders tried to topple them with long poles.

△ Knights use a siege tower and ladders to scale a castle's walls.

If they could not dig under or climb over the castle walls, attackers pounded them with battering rams. In 1216, besiegers battered the French castle of Beaucaire with an iron-tipped ram. But the defenders lowered down a rope noose and caught hold of the ram to stop it swinging.

▷ Norman troops swing a battering ram, protected by a fireproof cover called a 'cat' or 'sow'.

TOWER POWER

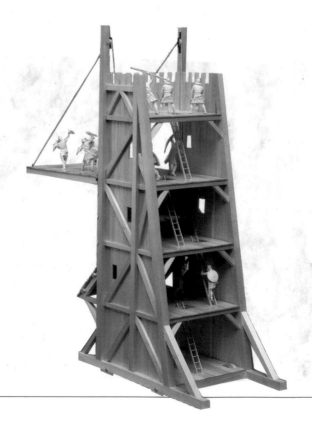

'The Franks built three wooden towers, each thirty metres high. They had five floors each crowded with soldiers. A special kind of wood was brought from abroad to build them. The towers were covered with wet hides, vinegar, mud and fire-resisting substances.'

The Deeds of Tancred, twelfth century.

BESIEGING

The commander rides out on his proud horse to look over the enemy fortifications. This is the third castle he has besieged in this summer's campaigning. He looks at the castle and frowns. It sits on a high rock and is defended by strong walls, towers and many lines of strong, sharpened stakes. If the castle has enough stores, the siege may last into winter.

△ Guidoriccio da Fogliano, the greatest commander in Italy, plans for a siege.

If tunnelling, bombarding, battering and scaling failed, the attackers resorted to besieging the castle. They surrounded its walls, and waited for the garrison to starve. Sometimes, they bribed the soldiers to give in. One garrison in a castle in Italy switched sides three times during a siege. Each time they were offered higher wages, they simply opened the castle gates.

◁ Edinburgh Castle, in Scotland, was the scene of many famous sieges.

Trickery also ended sieges. In 1341, Edinburgh Castle was held by the English. Surrounded by steep cliffs, it seemed safe from attack. However, the Scottish knight Sir William Douglas and his men disguised themselves as cloth merchants coming to trade. They stopped their wagons under the castle gates so the English could not close them. The Scottish army then rushed through and recovered the castle.

MAKE SIEGE BISCUITS

Ingredients: 200 g oatmeal, 1 teaspoon salt, 1 pinch bicarbonate of soda, 10-15 g fat.

1. Add salt and bicarbonate to oatmeal and mix well.
• Melt fat on a gentle heat and pour into oatmeal mix.
• Add enough water to make a soft dough. Knead well.

• Roll out the dough and cut into four circles.
• Lay the circles of dough on a baking tray sprinkled with some flour.

2. Cook for forty minutes at 150°C, Gas Mark 2.
• Leave to cool.
• Store in a safe place, where rats and weevils cannot find them. Eat only one a day. It may be a long siege.

THE DEFENCE

CASTLE DEFENCES

THE GARRISON MOUNT a furious defence of their castle. Rocks are dropped through trapdoors and red-hot sand bubbles in a cauldron, ready to be poured on to the besiegers. A knight's head bobs up over the battlements, but the defenders quickly push his ladder away.

The castle garrison used long, forked poles to force back enemy scaling ladders. Sir Edward Springhouse was toppled from his ladder at the siege of Caen in 1346. The French defenders then dropped burning straw on him and he was roasted alive in his armour.

Castle defenders often dropped roasting hot sand on to their attackers. The small grains of sand got under knights' armour, where it scorched and blistered their skin. Europeans learned this trick when on crusade.

GRAVENSTEEN

Gravensteen Castle, in Belgium, was built for the Count of Flanders in 1180. It has dozens of small projecting turrets. These were built so that crossbowmen could aim at every part of the ground below. They also made the castle look more impressive.

◁ Defenders fight back with arrows and rocks, and heat up a cauldron of sand.

FIGHTING BACK

The defenders on the battlements shake their fists and make a great noise. The besiegers below look up to see what is happening. Their attention is distracted. They do not see a secret 'postern' gate opening in the castle walls, and soldiers riding out past them. Soon, the besiegers' camp is in flames. Cheers go up from the castle battlements as their troops gallop back to safety.

There were many different ways to defend a castle. Carcassonne was once besieged until its defenders were starving. They filled the carcass of a pig with the last of their grain, and catapulted it over the walls. When it landed, the grain burst out. The attackers now believed that the garrison had such good stores that they could afford to feed grain to their pigs. So, they called off the siege.

△ The fortress city of Carcassonne in southern France.

The Italian writer Machiavelli noted in 1515: 'If a garrison stays in its fortress, it will surely starve. To break a siege it must harry the enemy, attack his camp, and use this distraction to send for help or food.'

◁ Trained archers used longbows to pick off careless besiegers.

△ The execution of Turkish spies at Rhodes in 1480.

FIRING ARROWS

Archers aimed their arrows at the enemy commanders. Longbows were also used to fire messages to friendly spies in the siege camp below. In 1387, Portuguese archers fired flaming arrows of cloth and tar which set fire to the enemy's tents.

Castle garrisons always had to watch for traitors and spies. In 1480, the Knights of St John were defending the island fortress of Rhodes in the Mediterranean. They executed several Turkish spies who were caught signalling to their friends in the siege camp outside.

SURVIVING

The siege has dragged on deep into the winter. Supplies are low. The hungry garrison queue at the castle kitchen for their meagre daily bowl of gruel. Others try to make a stew from rats and dead dogs. The castellan orders his men to throw out from the castle anyone who cannot fight.

During the siege of Castle Gaillard in 1204, the English garrison expelled the old and the sick. They were eating precious stores, but could not help defend the castle. The French king, Philip Augustus, refused to let these 'useless mouths' pass through his lines. They suffered a slow and horrible death, starving at the foot of the castle gates.

▽ Men on the battlements pretend to have food, as the starving garrison expel the 'useless mouths'.

A monk described a siege in around 1200: 'Valuable warhorses were slaughtered for their meat. Horse guts sold for ten shillings. Even noblemen begged for vegetables. Men ran about like mad dogs, crazed with hunger. They seized old dog bones and gnawed them for the pleasure of remembering the taste of meat.'

FOOD FIGHTS

Attackers as well as defenders suffered from hunger during a siege. These troops have mounted a strong guard on their supply wagons in case the occupants of the castle make a surprise raid and try to capture them.

FIGHTING BY THE RULES

RULES OF SIEGE

'O LORD, HAVE MERCY UPON US!' The starving garrison crawl out of the castle gates on their knees wearing the white gowns of penitents. They kneel before the king and ask for his forgiveness. He can choose to pardon them or execute them.

Rules of chivalry were normally followed during sieges, but some commanders disobeyed them. Attacking the Italian castle of Crema in 1160, Emperor Frederick Barbarossa of Germany tied captured relatives of the defenders to his siege tower. He thought this would stop the defenders setting fire to the tower, but he was wrong. The prisoners were burnt to death.

△ The rulers of a defeated city plead for mercy from the king who has defeated their forces.

▷ Stirling Castle, where armies agreed to end their siege on Midsummer's Day.

Many sieges ended peacefully because the armies agreed in advance a date to end the fighting. In 1314, the Scots were trying to recapture Stirling Castle. Sir Philip Mowbray, the English governor, promised to surrender the castle if no reinforcements reached him by Midsummer's Day. When his reinforcements were defeated at the Battle of Bannockburn, Mowbray kept his promise.

MAKE A SIEGE TRUCE

1. Crumple up a piece of plain paper, then straighten it out. Tear around the edges. Soak overnight in cold tea.

2. When it is dry, glue a rough circle of red Plasticine to your truce. Press a coin into the Plasticine to make your seal.

3. Use a fountain pen to write a list of the terms your enemy must follow before you surrender your castle.

SACK AND PILLAGE

'Sack the city!' Troops rush through the city looting and burning. They burst into the houses of merchants to search for gold and silver plate. The troops have not been paid but they can keep any treasure they find.

If a castle fell in a siege, the lord in charge of the besieging army could declare a 'sack'. This meant that his victorious soldiers could do anything they liked to their defeated enemy for three days. They could kill their prisoners and steal from them. Sometimes troops were allowed to 'sack' instead of being paid.

△ Crusaders sack the city of Jerusalem in 1099.

▷ Richard I watches as 2,700 Muslims are beheaded, during the sack of Acre in 1191.

When crusaders captured the city of Acre in 1191, King Richard promised not to execute the Muslim defenders if he received a ransom. When the ransom was not paid, Richard gave orders for the beheadings to start.

▽ Victorious attackers are offered the Koran as a gift after a successful siege.

If they could fight no longer, defenders offered religious relics, treasures, gold and precious books to the attackers' commander. If he was chivalrous, he took these goods and made a vow not to sack their homes.

NO MERCY

'The Black Prince had given orders to loot the city and kill the townsfolk, men, women and children. It was a terrible thing to see, families kneeling down in front of the Prince and asking for mercy.'

Jean Froissart describing the English sack of Limoges, France, 1370.

SIEGE IN THE HOLY LAND

CRUSADES

THE CRUSADER KNIGHTS glimpse the grim fortress walls of Jerusalem. They fall to their knees and thank God for bringing them to the Holy City. This is the sight they have longed for since setting off from Europe. Tomorrow, they will plan their attack on the Muslims who hold the city.

The crusades were campaigns fought in the hot, desert lands of Syria and Palestine. The only food and water was to be found in the walled cities which were held by the Muslims. To reach Jerusalem, the crusader armies had to lay siege to the castles and cities on the way.

△ The walls of Jerusalem, which the First Crusade reached in 1099.

▽ Crusaders launched attacks from land and sea at the siege of Antioch in 1098.

'The Franks came to an agreement with the commander of one of Antioch's towers, a breastplate maker called Firouz. The Franks promised him silver if he would betray the fortress to them.'

Ibn al-Athir, Arab chronicler, the siege of Antioch, 1098.

The crusaders besieged the city of Antioch for seven months. They bombarded it and attacked it with powerful siege towers but they could not breach the castle walls. Finally, they bribed a traitor called Firouz, who let the crusaders into the city at night.

During the siege of Antioch, the French priest Peter Bartholomew claimed to have discovered the Holy Lance. This was the spear used to torture Christ. Some knights believed it was a fake. To prove his honesty, Peter submitted to an 'ordeal of fire' – walking through a corridor of blazing logs. If he survived, he must be telling the truth. He died of his burns three days later.

▷ A crusader knight at prayer.

CONSTANTINOPLE

The fabulous churches and palaces of golden Constantinople nestle behind the strongest defences in the Christian world. Heralds blast their trumpets. The people of the city stand at the battlements and jeer at the Turkish besiegers below. For more than a thousand years, these walls have resisted all sieges.

Constantinople was founded in AD 303 by the Roman emperor Constantine. It was the largest, richest and strongest city in Christian Europe, and lay on the very edge of Muslim lands in Asia. The city was protected by sea on three sides, and walls over thirty metres high. It was besieged seven times by Muslims called Ottomans, but they failed to capture the city.

△ A painting of Constantinople's mighty walls, from a medieval book.

In 1453, the Ottomans besieged Constantinople once more. They were armed with cannon, including the Dardanelles Gun which is now in the Tower of London. This bronze cannon was so big it had to be transported in two halves, then screwed together. It could fire a missile weighing 300 kilograms over one-and-a-half kilometres.

△ A cannon used during the last siege of Constantinople.

The people of Constantinople thought they were safe behind their high walls. But within days, the Ottomans' powerful cannon had reduced the ancient defences to rubble. The Ottomans took over the city and gave it the Islamic name of Istanbul, which we still use today. Their victory showed how cannon could quickly bring a siege to an end.

◁ Ottoman chain mail, with words from the Koran engraved on the helmet.

37

GUNPOWDER SIEGES

BOMBARDS

'STAND BACK !' The master gunner steps up to light the bombard fuse then covers his ears. The gun roars and the stone shot flies towards its target. Then, he hears the groans. Men lie dying around him, pierced by shards of hot metal. The barrel of the bombard has shattered.

Cannons called 'bombards' were used in sieges after 1320. The first bombards overheated and burst if they were fired too often. Gunners had to wait up to six hours between shots to be safe from explosion. These early bombards' stone cannon balls often did not make much impact on well-designed castle walls.

▷ A fifteenth-century cannon called Mons Meg, cast in Belgium but used by the kings of Scotland.

The barrels of early bombards were made from strips of iron held together by tight metal hoops. If too much gunpowder was used, the force split the hoops apart. Later cannon were made from a single tube which was less likely to explode.

◁ Gunners argue and tend to their wounds after the explosion of their bombard.

USING THE NEW GUNS

The French king orders his gunners to begin the siege attack. They take aim and fire. A volley of iron cannon balls punch holes in the castle wall. Minutes later, another round of shots brings down the wall. After an hour, a herald rides out from the castle to offer the garrison's surrender.

In the 1490s, lightweight, bronze cannon were invented in France. They were set on wheels and easily pulled by horses. These cannon fired metal balls which could damage stone walls. In 1494, King Charles VIII of France used his new artillery to capture castles throughout Italy. The age of the knight living safely in his castle was over.

△ French kings used cannon to destroy the castles of powerful lords.

VIOLENT ENDS

'These cannons fired iron cannon balls which were heavier and more destructive than stone. These guns were so violent that they destroyed defences in hours which had previously held out in siege for many months.'

Francesco Guicciardini, sixteenth-century historian.

By 1500, engineers knew they had to build new kinds of fortress. High castle walls were too easy a target. New forts were built which had lower, thicker walls packed with earth and rubble. These were much harder to knock down.

▽ The fortress walls of Malta were reduced to rubble in the Great Siege of 1565.

▷ An army uses bows, handguns and cannon to force the surrender of a castle.

The new guns were also used at sea. In 1565, Ottoman ships besieged the island of Malta, cutting off the defenders' supplies. Malta's defences were badly damaged by the Ottoman cannon, but a Christian fleet arrived just in time to save the island.

THE END OF AN AGE

THE KING LOOKS DOWN on the battlefield, and plots the siege of the city. Siege tents surround the fortified walls. The royal cannon concentrate their bombardment on one area. Musketeers keep up a steady fire, so that the defenders have to keep their heads down and cannot repair the damage to their walls.

After 1500, cannon were used to enforce royal power. Proud cities like Chartres in France were forced to obey the king, and had their walls reduced to rubble to make sure that they did. The phrase 'The King's last word' was engraved on the French royal cannon.

△ Batteries of cannon surround the city of Chartres in 1568.

▽ Built as a castle, the Alcazar is now a magnificent palace.

The coming of guns meant there was little point in building castles for defence. The Alcazar in Spain was originally a castle. After 1500, its owners continued to build towers and battlements, but these were for display not defence. Like many castles across Europe, the Alcazar was turned into a magnificent palace. The age of castle life, knights and sieges was over.

TIMELINE

390 BC	212 BC	AD 1098	1099
The Gauls besiege Rome's Capitol.	Archimedes invents new siege weapons during the Siege of Syracuse.	Crusaders bombard Nicaea with the heads of their Turkish prisoners.	Jerusalem is besieged and sacked by Christian knights.

1204		1215	1240
King Philip Augustus of France captures Chateau Gaillard after a long siege.	Crusaders sack the Christian city of Constantinople.	Rochester Castle in Kent, England, is besieged by King John for over fifty days.	Carcassonne in France is saved by a dead pig stuffed with grain.

1370		1450	1453
The Black Prince slaughters his prisoners during the sack of Limoges.		The giant bombard Mons Meg is made in Belgium and shipped to Edinburgh.	Ottoman Turks use bombards to breach the walls of Constantinople.

1160	1190	1191
Emperor Frederick Barbarossa orders tortures at the Siege of Crema in Italy. 	Richard the Lionheart orders the building of Chateau Gaillard in Normandy.	Acre in the Holy Land is sacked by knights of the First Crusade.

1300	1341	1346	1350
Siege engineers begin to use gunpowder to blow up castles.	Scots use trickery to recapture Edinburgh Castle from the English.	Diseased corpses are fired over walls at the siege of Tana in Russia.	Cannon are used in the sieges of castles in France and Burgundy.

1494	1550	
Accurate bronze cannon used by the French end the age of castles.	Castle walls are replaced by low earth walls which absorb the impact of cannonballs.	

allies Groups of people who help each other, especially at war.

bailey The outer courtyard of a castle.

Bohemia A kingdom in central Europe.

bombardment Constant launching of missiles at a castle.

booty Treasure won at war.

breach Make a gap in a castle wall.

breastplate A piece of armour protecting the chest.

bribed Given money to do something you should not.

brine Salted water for preserving meat.

carcass The dead body of an animal.

cauldron A metal pot used for cooking.

Celtic Belonging to an ancient race of people from western Europe.

chain mail Armour made from linked rings of metal.

chivalry Rules of behaviour followed by a knight.

crusaders People who fought holy wars in the Middle East.

drawbridge A bridge lowered over a castle moat to allow entry.

embrasures Narrow slits in castle walls for archers to fire through.

Flanders A medieval region in the lowlands of western Europe.

Franks People from Europe, especially Germany, fighting in the Middle East.

garrison The soldiers stationed at a castle.

Gauls An ancient Celtic people who lived in what is now France.

gruel A thin soup made from boiling oatmeal in water.

harry Worry, harass, make occasional attacks on an enemy.

keep The central tower of a castle, usually built of stone.

Koran The holy book of the Muslims.

mason A skilled craftsman who built castles out of stone.

motte The steep hill which was the main part of an early Norman castle.

Muslims Followers of the Islamic religion, who lived in Spain, North Africa and the Middle East in medieval times.

penitents People who publicly ask for forgiveness for their sins.

portcullis A strong gate of crossed bars lowered to guard a castle gateway.

postern A side door or entrance.

ramparts Castle walls, usually with a walkway at the top.

serfs Peasants not allowed to leave the lord's land on which they worked.

shillings An old form of coins.

winch A wooden crank used for tightening ropes on catapults.

FURTHER INFORMATION

PLACES TO VISIT

WALES

Cardiff Castle's Norman keep was besieged and stormed by the Welsh in 1158. **Caerphilly Castle** was besieged many times between 1270 and 1500. A working portcullis can be seen at **Oystermouth Castle** near Swansea.

SCOTLAND

A reconstructed mangonel sits in the grounds of **Caerlaverock Castle** near Dumfries. Edinburgh's **Craigmillar Castle** has excellent 'machicolations' once used for dropping missiles on to enemies. The bombard Mons Meg is exhibited inside **Edinburgh Castle**.

ENGLAND

Leeds Castle in Kent, protected by its wide moat, is still used for government meetings. **Warwick Castle** began as a Norman motte but by 1500 had 'a mighty tower of strengthe, for to shoute out gunns'. The stone keep at **Rochester** in Kent was besieged three times; in 1088 by Rufus, 1215 by John I and in 1264 by Simon de Montfort. After a siege of over six months in 1266, the defenders of **Kenilworth**, Warwickshire, were allowed to leave with the full honours of war. **Clifford's Tower** in York stands on the site of one of the earliest Norman castles in England.

BOOKS

Arms and Armour, Michele Byam
(Dorling Kindersley, 2003)
Best Ever Book of Castles,
Philip Steele (Kingfisher, 1997)
Castle, C. Gravett
(Dorling Kindersley, 2002)
Scottish Castles Through History
Richard Dargie (Wayland, 1998)

INDEX